COMPONENTS
&
CONDITIONS

The Pocket Guide to Strategy Consulting Case
Interviews and Estimation Questions

Edward Vernon

Copyright © 2019 Edward Vernon

All rights reserved.

ISBN-13: 9781697646719

ACKNOWLEDGMENTS

As with most endeavors of progression, I stand heavily on the shoulders of the writers and academics who came before me. Acknowledgement is deserved by Michael Porter, Victor Cheng and Marc P. Consentino for forming the foundational knowledge for how I think about strategic problem-solving.

I also want to thank Matthew Ives , an ex-McKinsey consultant, who first recommended I explore the strategy consulting profession, along with Mark Daley, Melody Goh and Rachel Tonner from the Imperial College Business School careers team for practicing a ridiculous number of cases with me while I was studying for my master's degree.

Finally, a special thanks goes to my colleagues currently working at the world's leading strategy consulting firms for encouraging me to write this book and advising on its content.

CONTENTS

1 OVERVIEW 1

2 CASE INTERVIEWS 3

Case Interview Fundamentals 3

How to Structure Your Notes 4

Component Trees and Condition Trees 5

'Problem / Solution Identification' vs 'Should We?' Questions and the Role of the Hypothesis 7

Problem/Solution Identification Questions: 7

Should We? Questions: 8

No Matter the Question, Always Check Client Alignment: 9

Framework Approach Examples: 9

The Case Interview Process 10

Ensure your Branches are MECE 11

Introduction to MECE Structures: 11

How to Achieve a MECE Structure: 13

Core Frameworks and How They Relate 18

The Profitability Component Tree 18

Why Average Price May Have Dropped . 20

How to Increase the Average Price 20

Why Sales Quantity May Have Dropped 21

How to Increase the Sales Quantity 21

Why Fixed Costs May Have Increased ... 25

How to Decrease the Fixed Costs 25

Why Variable Costs May Have Increased 26

How to Decrease the Variable Cost per Unit 26

Target Sourcing & Prioritisation 26

Market Entry into New Products or New Geographies 27

COMPONENTS & CONDITIONS

- Mergers & Acquisitions 30
- Key Case Interview Principles 33
- Scenarios to Watch Out For 36
  - Independence of Quantity Sold and Variable Cost 36
  - The Mix Effect 37

3 ESTIMATION QUESTIONS 38

- Geometric Estimation Questions 39
- Market Sizing 44

5 GENERAL TIPS 47

6 EXAMPLE CASE 49

1
OVERVIEW

If you are applying to strategy consulting firms like I was back in 2018, you will undoubtedly hear about the specific techniques these firms use to interview candidates. The case interview, along with estimation questions, comprises the cornerstone of the assessment process for nearly all these firms.

When starting to read about case interviews over the summer before starting business school, it sounded simple enough. However, I spent a significant amount of time confused over how to implement the techniques I had read about when it came to practising cases later that year.

I, therefore, decided to take what I had learned and develop my own methodology for solving cases and estimation questions, one that made logical sense to me and ultimately led me to land a strategy consulting role at one of London's top firms. These techniques helped me enormously along with my classmates at business school with whom I shared and practised them.

The reason for me writing this book is to share what I have learned, build on the previous literature surrounding case interviews and hopefully help fellow candidates use effective methodologies to excel in this unique type of interview.

Throughout this book will cover the two types of questions independently; first case interviews and then estimation questions. I will give guidance on methodologies and frameworks you can use to form the foundational knowledge required to ask the right questions and clearly structure your thoughts.

I must stress that these frameworks are simply a guide and if there is one thing I learnt from my interview practice it's that a candidate must mould their techniques to their own way of thinking along with the specific case at hand.

Furthermore, I would recommend using this book as a supplement to more extensive pieces of writing on case interviews such as 'Case Interview Secrets' by Victor Cheng which covers the context of why these interviews exist, what interviewers are looking for and the foundational knowledge of the issue tree problem-solving methodology.

2
CASE INTERVIEWS

Case Interview Fundamentals

This book focuses purely on specific techniques for tackling strategy consulting case interviews. These types of cases, focused on topics such as profitability, M&A and market entry, are the problems you are likely to receive at core strategy consulting firms such as McKinsey, BCG, Bain, Monitor Deloitte, EY-Parthenon and OC&C, along with the specialised strategy teams at more generalist firms such as Accenture and PA Consulting Group.

It is worth bearing in mind however, that some of the larger strategy consulting firms such as McKinsey are starting to move into more operational areas and hence these applicants may also receive operational case interviews. I would recommend all strategy consulting applicants to become comfortable with operational cases to ensure they cover all bases although it should not be the focus of their preparation if they are applying to 'pure strategy' houses.

The case interview fundamentals we will cover apply to all strategic and operational cases. However, the specific frameworks covered later are focused exclusively on strategic problems.

How to Structure Your Notes

If a client does not understand how you have arrived at the recommendation you give them, they are unlikely to trust it. This goes for case interviewers as well. Making it clear how you have arrived at the answer you give is just as important, if not more important than the answer itself. One of the best ways to achieve this is by laying your notes out in a clear way. Interviewers will often take a candidate's notes away with them after the interview to assess as part of their appraisal of your performance so it is vital they can understand what they are looking at.

Below is how I divide up my paper at the start of a case interview. If there is a heavy focus on a particular area, such as calculations, feel free to continue this work on a separate piece of paper.

COMPONENTS & CONDITIONS

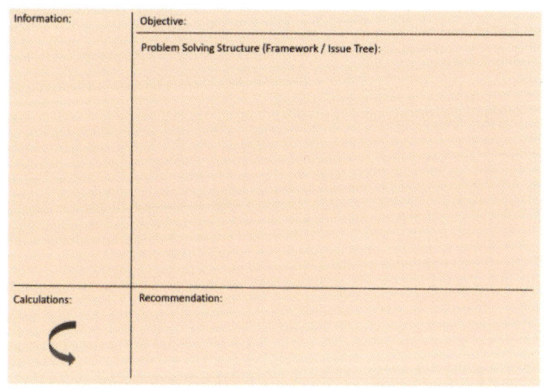

Figure 1: A4 Case Layout

Component Trees and Condition Trees

The core method through which a strategy consultant solves their client's problems is through a series of problem subdivisions called a framework. In its simplest form, the typical consulting framework consists of a set of guesses ('hypotheses' in consulting terminology) to the question being asked, followed by a list of all the information required to know whether each guess is true or false.

This first set of guesses comprises all the possible drivers of the client's problem and is known as a component tree. The following list of information required to prove or disprove the hypothesis that a particular component is the cause of the problem is known as a condition tree (conditions which must be true for the hypothesis to be true).

A candidate should use component and condition trees in an iterative way, focusing on their 'best guess', or hypothesis, first, testing it against the available data with a condition tree and proceeding if it is found to be true or revising it to their next best guess and repeating the process if it is found to be false. The condition trees used to test each hypothesis should also be prioritised according to the importance of the conditions.

This technique of focusing on your 'best guess', or hypothesis, first along with prioritising the conditions to test it, improves a consultant's efficiency in solving a problem, avoiding the need to look at every piece of information before making a recommendation to a client.

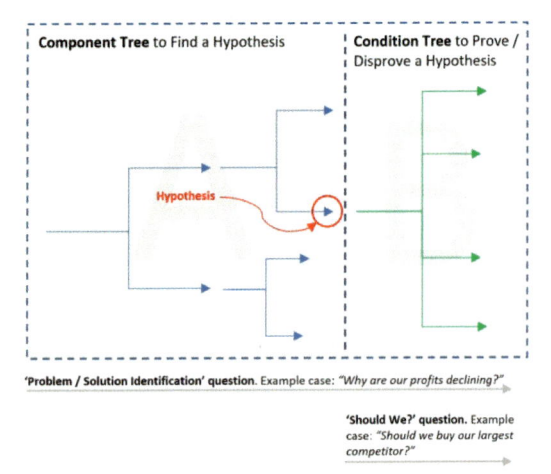

Figure 2: Component and Condition Trees for 'Problem/Solution Identification' vs 'Should We?' Questions

'Problem / Solution Identification' vs 'Should We?' Questions and the Role of the Hypothesis

Interviewers will generally expect for a candidate to state their hypothesis within the first 5 minutes of a case ('the five-minute rule'). An important consideration however when using a hypothesis is that there are two overarching types of questions that can be asked by an interviewer that determine how a hypothesis should be used and what type of problem-solving tree should be built. I call these 'should we?' questions and 'problem/solution identification' questions.

Problem/Solution Identification Questions:

When solving a 'Problem/Solution Identification' question, a candidate should design a component tree, outlining all the components which drive the negative phenomena with which the client is concerned. Following this, the candidate should choose what they feel is the most likely driver of the problem and state this as their hypothesis. Interviewers generally look for this hypothesis to be stated early on, adhering to the '5-minute rule' after possibly a few clarifying questions. This process, as discussed, helps narrow down the areas of analysis, ensuring the areas most likely to hold the answer to the case are examined first. Following the hypothesis, the candidate should build a condition tree, outlining the various conditions that need to be true to prove the hypothesis.

Should We? Questions:

It is important to understand that a 'Should We?' question, on the other hand, is a 'problem/solution identification' question where the interviewer has already chosen your hypothesis for you. Within an M&A case question of 'Should we acquire company X?' for example, the hypothesis chosen for you is the client's guess that the best method of achieving their goals is through an acquisition. The candidate's job, in this case, is simply to prove or disprove this hypothesis with a condition tree.

In a 'Should we?' case a hypothesis holds little value early on as it does not help prioritise the areas of analysis. For example; if asked whether your client should acquire a competitor, you will always examine the same areas of feasibility, then target, then synergies and finally risks in that order. We will discuss this framework in more detail later however, in this type of case, a hypothesis that the client should or should not proceed with the acquisition does not assist with prioritising your analysis. No matter your initial feeling about what the answer should be, you will still look at exactly the same areas in the same order. Therefore, a hypothesis should not be stated for this type of question unless explicitly asked to by the interviewer.

If given a 'Should We?' question, a candidate should start at the point of the hypothesis and builds a condition tree straight away.

COMPONENTS & CONDITIONS

No Matter the Question, Always Check Client Alignment:

With both 'Problem/Solution Identification' and 'Should We?' questions, a candidate should always check that their problem structure and prioritisation is aligned with how the client thinks about a problem. In most cases, the client will know more about their industry than the consultant, so it is important to be humble and ensure that you leverage their knowledge to help structure your case.

For a 'Problem/Solution Identification' question, this may sound like; "I have split the problem into its components of A, B, C and D. My initial hypothesis is that C is the root cause of this issue so I would like to look at this area first if that's okay with you? It would also be helpful to check that this structure is aligned with how you think about the problem?"

For a 'Should We?' question, this may sound like; "In order to understand whether it is a good idea for you to X, I've outlined several conditions that are crucial for its success. These would be A, B, C and D. I would first like to look at C as I feel this is the most critical factor if that's okay with you? It would also be helpful to check that these conditions are aligned with how you think about the problem?"

Framework Approach Examples:

- "Our profits have been dropping. Why?"
  o   Full-stack (Component tree > Hypothesis -> Condition Tree)
- "Should we enter the Australian market?"

9

- o Condition Tree Only
- • "Which market should we next expand to?"
- o Full-stack (Component tree -> Hypothesis -> Condition Tree)
- • "Should we shut down our manufacturing facility and outsource this activity instead?"
- o Condition tree only

The Case Interview Process

When practising for case interviews, it is important to become comfortable with a process that can help guide you to a final recommendation. Due to the subtle differences between 'Problem/Solution Identification' and 'Should We?' questions, this process differs slightly. Below are the processes I aim to stick to when solving each type of case.

Problem / Solution Identification Questions:
1. Note down information
2. Clarify information and request any more background information if needed
3. Clarify the objective and that there are no other objectives
4. Create a structure to find your hypothesis (component tree)
5. Explain your structure, state your hypothesis and ensure alignment
6. Design a testing structure (condition tree)
7. Ask for information
8. Analyse the information
9. Revise hypothesis if necessary and go back to step 6
10. Write out your recommendation

COMPONENTS & CONDITIONS

11. State recommendation and explain why you are giving it
12. State what you would look at further if you had more time

Should We? Questions:
1. Note down information
2. Clarify information and request any more background information if needed
3. Clarify the objective and that there are no other objectives
4. Design a testing structure (condition tree)
5. Explain your structure, state priorities and ensure alignment
6. Ask for information
7. Analyse information
8. Write your recommendation
9. State your recommendation and explain why you are giving it
10. State what you would look at further if you had more time

Ensure your Branches are MECE

Introduction to MECE Structures:

An important consideration when constructing a problem-solving tree is to ensure that all of your branches are mutually exclusive and collectively exhaustive (MECE). This principle is most important for component trees; however, a MECE aspiration for condition trees will also be valuable but sometimes may not be possible.

MECE branches contain no overlaps (mutually exclusive) and together cover all relevant areas of analysis (collectively exhaustive). MECE branches ensure that the components of a logical argument do not contradict each other and that no relevant areas are left out of the analysis.

The MECE principle should be applied to all branches that share a common origin. In computer science, from which problem-solving trees developed, these branches are known as siblings. Think; all children that share the same parent, and hence are siblings, must together be MECE.

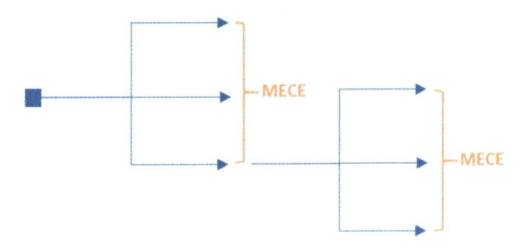

Figure 3: MECE Branches

The following example of where to go on holiday demonstrates the issues with a component tree not being MECE:

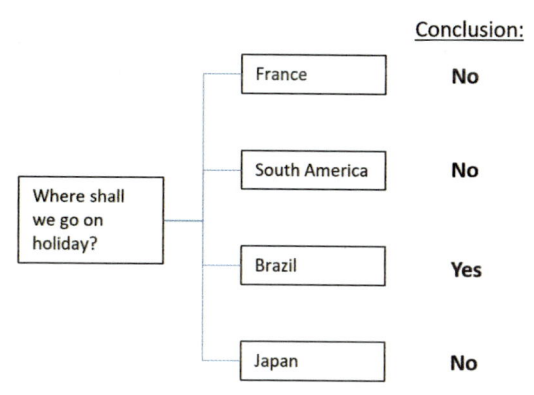

Figure 4: Non-MECE Example

In this example, the branches are neither mutually exclusive nor collectively exhaustive. Because of this, two issues arise:

1. Because the branches are not mutually exclusive, there is the contradiction of a conclusion of going to Brazil but not going to South America.

2. Because the branches are not collectively exhaustive the decision to visit Brazil is taken without considering Italy, for example, which could have been an even better option.

How to Achieve a MECE Structure:
Mathematical Structures

When required to solve a numerical problem such as 'why has X reduced?' or 'how can we increase Y?', a useful way to structure your problem-solving tree is to break down the metric being examined into its mathematical components.

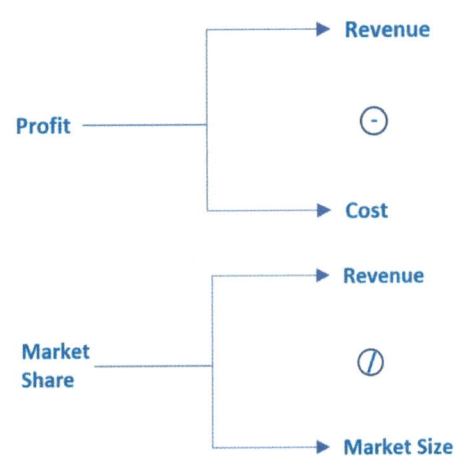

Figure 5: Example Mathematical MECE Structures

Process Structures

Often, when required to solve a 'problem/solution identification' case that has an underlying process, breaking the problem into the individual steps of the process is the best way to achieve a MECE structure. An example case ideal for a process structure would be when tasked to identify the cause of a variable cost increase for the product your client manufactures. Other areas where process structures could be useful include hiring processes, sales processes and other manufacturing problems.

I would suggest looking at Porter's Value Chain as a great starting point for understanding what steps may be involved in a strategically important process.

Conceptual Structures

The third MECE technique when building a problem-solving tree is achieved through grouping similar topics together into a common concept to then analyse independently. This technique requires more thought to ensure it is MECE as gaps and overlaps are not automatically avoided as they are in mathematical or process structures. Therefore, if it is possible to use a mathematical or process structure, this would be the preferred option.

Many useful frameworks have previously been developed using the conceptual approach which can be a great way to start thinking about many different cases.

Three basic conceptual frameworks I would recommend looking at are; Porter's Five Forces, used to assess the attractiveness of an industry; 3Cs, used to assess how well a company will perform in a competitive environment; and the 4Ps, used to understand the most important considerations when marketing a new product.

Segmentation

As an alternative to conceptual frameworks, when mathematical equations and process structures cannot be used, a candidate can instead segment the drivers of the problem by a chosen criterion. This criterion can be anything from sector to geographic region or socio-economic status.

Segmentation has the benefit of always being MECE as you are simply splitting up the original problem into smaller pieces. It, however, has the downside of offering no insight into the root cause of a problem as it tracks the same metric as the initial problem. It should, therefore only be used to complement other MECE techniques.

Conceptual Opposites

The final MECE technique when building an issue tree is through using two branches which correspond to opposite drivers. For example; internal factors vs external factors, or, supply issues vs demand issues.

Bear in mind that when building a problem-solving tree, you can combine multiple MECE techniques into one framework. You must, however, stick to one MECE technique across the branches that share a common origin.

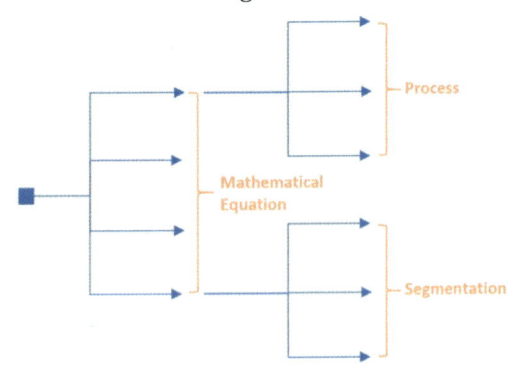

Figure 6: Example of Different MECE techniques Across the Same Tree

COMPONENTS & CONDITIONS

Many thanks to the team at CraftingCases (2017) for the inspiration for this section on MECE structures. I would highly recommend checking out their website and YouTube channel as a fantastic further resource for framework design.

Core Frameworks and How They Relate

Over the next few chapters, I will aim to provide an interconnected set of frameworks that I feel provide a great foundational set of knowledge to begin tackling strategy-based case interviews. These will by no means provide a 'plug and play' solution whereby memorising them will be enough. However, they should provide insight into the kind of structures and considerations a candidate should be thinking about throughout a case interview.

Each framework in this section continues from the next, creating a full-length process, from top-level profitability issues to actionable strategy. Case interviews do not typically cover such a lengthy process although I feel it would be helpful to see how all the frameworks you may have heard about elsewhere relate to one another.

The Profitability Component Tree

The profitability framework is the most well-known of all case interview frameworks. It uses simple mathematical equations to break down the various components of profit and is the perfect place

COMPONENTS & CONDITIONS

to start for any profitability-related case problem.

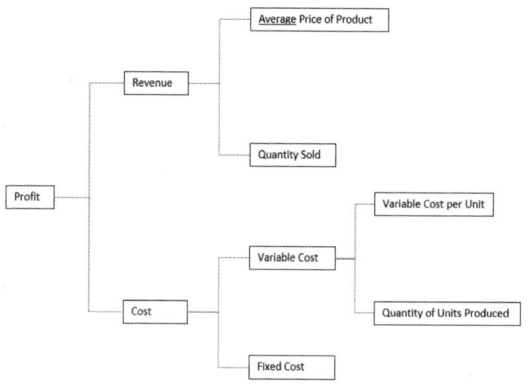

Figure 7: Profitability Tree

This framework, designed to understand the reason for a drop in a company's profits and how they can be improved, is the fundamental basis of every strategic decision made by a for-profit business. Every strategic case, from market entry to outsourcing, is driven by profit motivation. It is, therefore, important to understand how the profitability framework works and why all other frameworks build from it.

An extremely important clarifying question to make at the beginning of a profitability case, if it is at all unclear, is whether the issue the client is concerned about is a drop in their net profit or profit margin. If profit margin is the issue, the candidate must be aware that the metric in question is profit as a percentage of revenues rather than a standalone number. There are plenty of cases in which net profits have increased; however, the profit margin has decreased. It crucial you understand with which metric the client is concerned.

In profitability cases, a candidate will often be required to identify the root cause of the problem and then propose a solution. Below are some examples of why each of the key components of profitability may be underperforming along with some strategies to reverse these effects.

Why Average Price May Have Dropped

1. Product Mix Effect:

One of the most common reasons for average price to have dropped in a case is what is known as the 'mix effect'. This phenomenon occurs when there are proportional changes in the number of different types of products being sold. Refer to page 37 for more information on the 'mix effect'.

2. Response to Industry Price War.
3. Instigation of Industry Price War.
4. Response to Drop in Demand.

How to Increase the Average Price

Overall, raising the price of a product is challenging and usually requires specialised marketing knowledge. Thankfully, few cases focus on pricing strategies; however, it is essential to have basic knowledge of how pricing can be manipulated effectively.

Some ideas on how to increase the price of a product without losing significant demand for it:

1. If the demand for a product is price inelastic*, raise the price.

COMPONENTS & CONDITIONS

2. Change the product mix – sell proportionally more high-priced products.

3. Implement a forward integration strategy, raising the price at which you sell the product to the next participant in the value chain. (Conduct profit pool analysis to help decide which segment of the value chain to grow in to.)

4. Launch promotional campaigns designed to create a premium perception of the product.

5. Implement psychological pricing strategies. (Look at the compromise effect and asymmetric dominance effect).

6. Implement price discrimination.

Why Sales Quantity May Have Dropped

1. Demand Problem

Conditions:

- Sales of comparable products from competitors have also dropped.
- Increase in inventory.

2. Supply Problem

Conditions:

- Sales of comparable products are stable.
- Production quantity has reduced.

How to Increase the Sales Quantity

Whether coming from a profitability case, a revenue problem case or simply a quantity problem, candidates will often be tasked with finding the best way to increase the quantity of the products their client sells.

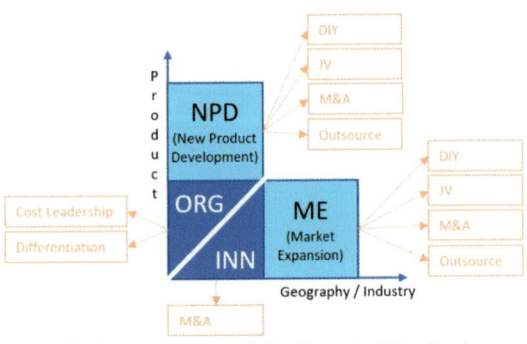

Figure 8: How to Increase Sales Quantity Visualisation

I find the best way to structure this problem is to use a conceptual structure to look at the question of 'what will the client be selling?' and 'where will the client be selling it?'. The resulting possible strategies are as follows:

Firstly, the company can try to sell more of the same product in the same market. This strategy, represented by the dark blue square, is the preferred option as it leverages the company's core capabilities and expertise. This strategy can be further split into organic and inorganic growth. Organic growth can be achieved by attracting customers through either lower prices (cost leadership) or a differentiated product / promotional message (differentiation). Inorganic growth, on the other hand, is achieved through mergers and acquisitions (M&A).

Secondly, the company can broaden its product offering, developing new products to sell in the same market. Finally, the company can attempt to sell its current product offering to a new market either, a new geographic region or, for B2B companies, a new industry.

Of course, it is also possible to adopt a strategy in the top right corner, developing a new product for a new market. However, this is typically a very high-risk approach given the large number of uncertainties.

In implementing this framework, a candidate or consultant must first determine whether competing with the current product in the current market or branching out into the NPD or ME areas is the optimal growth strategy for their client. They then can tackle how specifically to compete or which market or product to enter as a separate question. Consider the following framework:

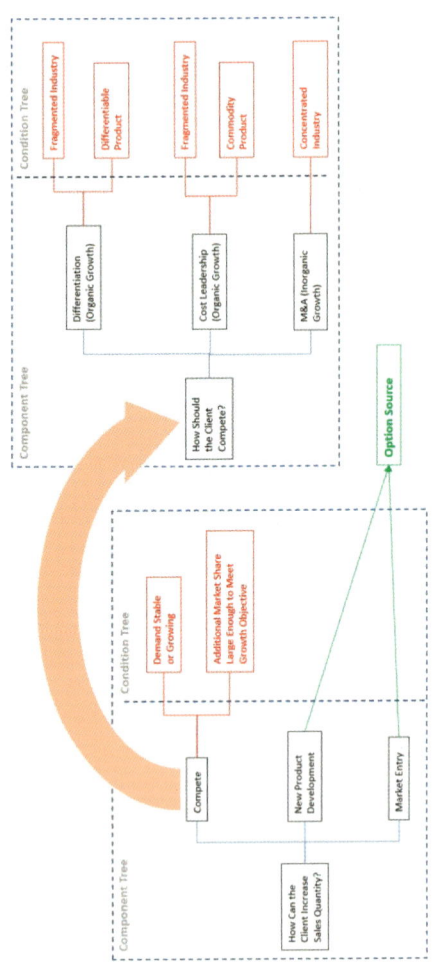

Figure 9: How to Increase Sales Quantity Component/Condition Trees

As you can see, I have split up the questions of how to increase sales quantity and how to compete into two separate problem-solving trees. This is a useful approach when solving questions that are conceptually quite different.

If, on the other hand, it is determined that a growth strategy into another product or market would be most effective, the process of target sourcing should be undertaken next which we will cover on the following two pages.

Why Fixed Costs May Have Increased

1. Increase in indirect supplier power (unionised labour, merger, etc.).
2. Change in an indirect supplier.
3. Increased demand for supporting activity assets.

How to Decrease the Fixed Costs

Fixed costs are typically challenging to manipulate (their name being a giveaway); however, over the long run, there are a few strategies that can be effective in reducing them.

1. Renegotiate indirect wages.
2. Renegotiate rent.
3. Reduce or sublet rented space.
4. Move facilities to a cheaper region for wages or rent.
5. Outsource support activities in the value chain.
6. Down-skill indirect workforce.
7. Shrink indirect workforce.

8. Automate indirect workforce.

Why Variable Costs May Have Increased

1. Product Mix Effect

As discussed on price, the proportional sales of a company's products can also impact its variable costs. If a company starts selling proportionally more of a more expensive product to produce, it's variable costs will increase. Refer to chapter x for more details.

2. Increased demand for raw materials.
3. Increased demand for direct labour.
4. Increase in supplier power (unionised labour, merger etc.)
5. Change in supplier.
6. Change in material specifications.

How to Decrease the Variable Cost per Unit

1. Renegotiate costs.
2. Change suppliers.
3. Backward integration.
4. Change location of labour force
5. Automation

Target Sourcing & Prioritisation

As discussed earlier, candidates and consultants can find themselves in a position where they know they should pursue a particular strategy, such as develop a new product, enter a new market or buy a competing company, however, they now need to determine which particular product, market or company they should pursue.

COMPONENTS & CONDITIONS

This situation is where target sourcing comes into play. This technique is used when picking a certain market, product, customer segment or company to target as part of a strategy. It involves understanding what criteria is of most importance to the client and then plotting the possible options against them.

For example, if looking for geographic expansion options, the criteria of analysis are likely to be market size and demand growth rate. A candidate should then plot the various countries likely to hold potential for this expansion strategy against the chosen criteria, pick the highest-ranking option and then assess it according to a market entry framework which we shall look at next.

Market Entry into New Products or New Geographies

When needing to prove or disprove a hypothesis that a company should enter a new market or develop a new product, I recommend building a prioritised condition tree based on the following visualisation:

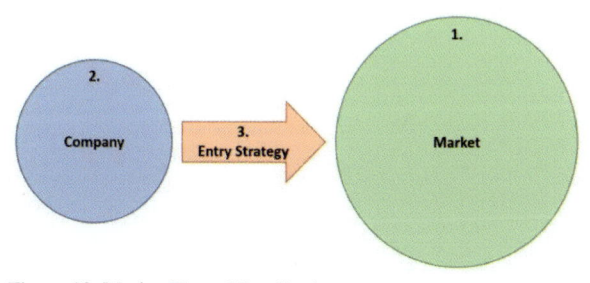

Figure 10: Market Entry Visualisation

The logic of this prioritisation is that if the market or product category is not attractive, we can end the analysis there and look for an alternative. If it is found to be attractive, we will now want to know if the company is capable of entering this market and if it is aligned with their current positioning. Finally, if it late-career that the company has the capability and alignment required to enter the market, we should now determine the best possible entry strategy.

COMPONENTS & CONDITIONS

Should Client Enter This Market?

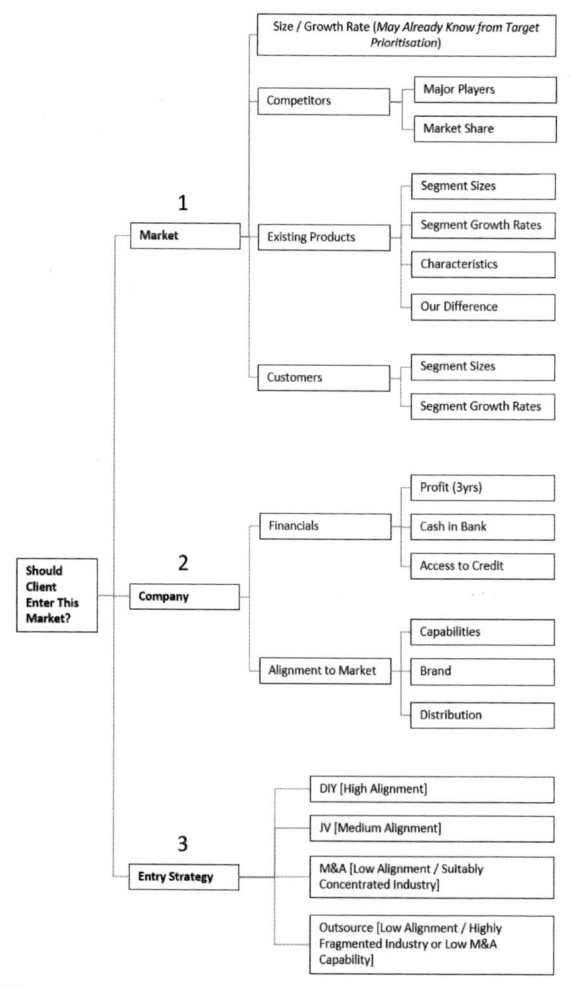

1. Market
- Size / Growth Rate (*May Already Know from Target Prioritisation*)
- Competitors
  - Major Players
  - Market Share
- Existing Products
  - Segment Sizes
  - Segment Growth Rates
  - Characteristics
  - Our Difference
- Customers
  - Segment Sizes
  - Segment Growth Rates

2. Company
- Financials
  - Profit (3yrs)
  - Cash in Bank
  - Access to Credit
- Alignment to Market
  - Capabilities
  - Brand
  - Distribution

3. Entry Strategy
- DIY [High Alignment]
- JV [Medium Alignment]
- M&A [Low Alignment / Suitably Concentrated Industry]
- Outsource [Low Alignment / Highly Fragmented Industry or Low M&A Capability]

Figure 11: Market Entry Condition Tree

All growth activities outside of your current product-market fit (NPD and ME) can be achieved either through a do-it-yourself approach, joint venture, M&A or through outsourcing. A logical approach in assessing which entry strategy is optimal for the client is to base the decision on the level of alignment between the client and the market or product they plan to enter/develop.

Mergers & Acquisitions

Similarly, when required to assess whether a company should acquire or merge with another company, use an M&A framework to prove or disprove the particular hypothesis you make or that is given to you. I have provided an example framework for both corporate M&A and private equity cases in figures 12 and 13.

Remember that the market entry and M&A frameworks are condition trees designed for testing a hypothesis. If you are solving a 'Problem/Solution Identification' question and your analysis shows that the chosen market or company is not the optimal target, the hypothesis should be revised to the next best option and assessed again.

COMPONENTS & CONDITIONS

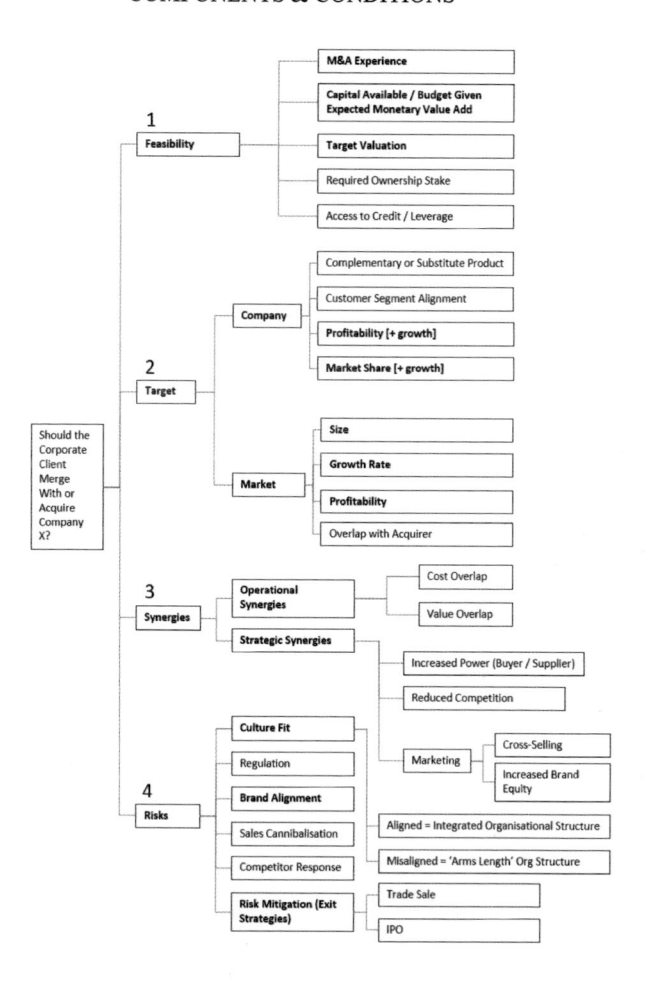

Figure 12: Corporate Mergers and Acquisitions (M&A) Condition Tree

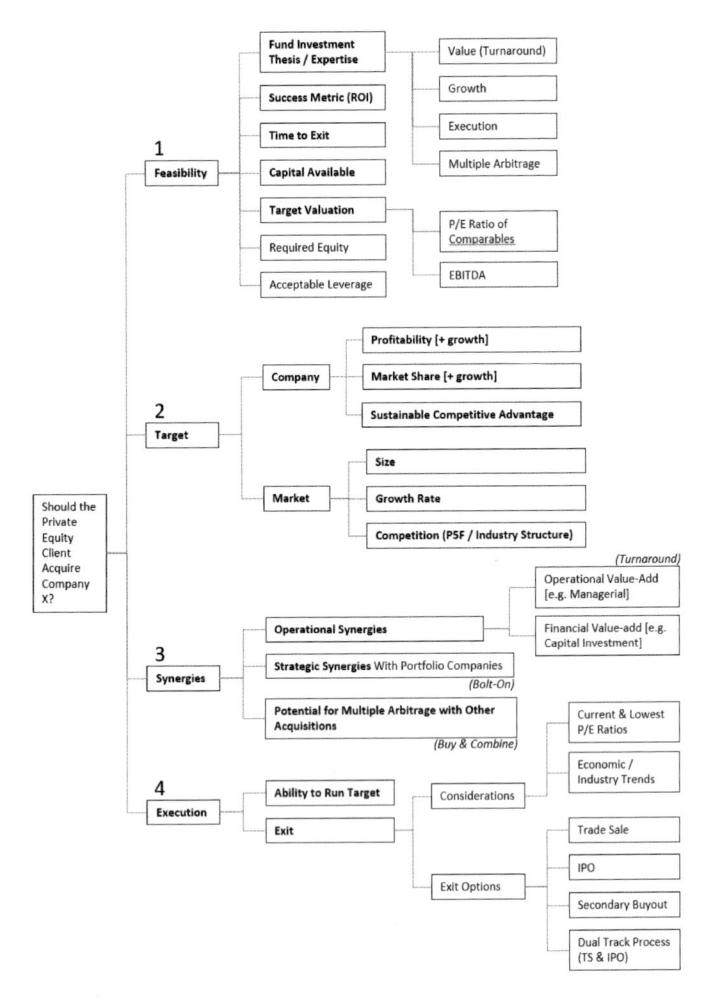

Figure 13: Private Equity Acquisitions Condition Tree

Key Case Interview Principles

Treat your Interviewer as if They are Your Client

This is one of the most important principles in case interviewing. Treating your interviewer as if you are already a consultant and they are your client helps with every aspect of the case. Putting yourself in this mindset will help guide the kind of questions you ask, how you ask them and how you communicate your findings. Furthermore, it will boost your points in the important assessment criteria of 'client readiness'.

At the start of a case, even when practising, I recommend making a mental note to put yourself in the position of a consultant advising a client. This reframing can be hard when many interviewers at the start of a case say, "Your client is X company…", speaking about the client in the third person. In this case, try to mentally rephrase what they have said to "I am X company…" and clarify that you will be assuming they are playing the role of the client.

If in Doubt, Drill Down

If ever you get stuck in a case where there seems to be going on, but it's unclear why; drill down further into a problem by creating another level of the issue tree, further segmenting the problem into its component parts.

An example would be variable costs: If it is unclear why the average variable cost per unit is rising, segment the cost further into each different type of product the client sells.

Ask for Likely Pre-Made Segmentations

If the client has likely already segmented a certain component, ask for this segmentation. Examples would be cost breakdown, product mix and customer segments.

It is inefficient to design a certain structure which then must be edited following the realisation that it is different from how the client's data is segmented.

Use Your Own Knowledge and Insight

Bringing your own knowledge into a case interview to help guide your analysis is looked upon very well by interviewers. Of course, this knowledge should only help to guide you in prioritising what to look at, rather than form the actual basis of your recommendation.

Ask for Specific Information

Most cases will require candidates to extract information from the interviewer to help solve the case interview problem. Many candidates at this stage fall into the trap of being too general when asking for this information. You should treat this process as you would when requesting information from a client – if they don't specifically know what you want, they won't know what to give you.

For example; in a profitability problem, the

candidate may make an initial hypothesis that the fall in profit is down to a cost issue. A bad request, often made by candidates, would be; "Do you have any information on costs?". In this case, the candidate is treating the interviewer like an interviewer, guessing at what information they have on their side of the table. Asking a client if they have any information on costs would be bizarre as every company is required to keep track of their accounts, costs being a major component.

Instead, a good request would be "If possible, may I have a breakdown of your variable costs over the last three years?". In this case, the client would know exactly what numbers to bring you and over what time period.

As a general rule, you want to avoid an interviewer or client replying to your request; "What specifically would you like to know?". If this happens, you have been to general.

Practise!

There is no substitute for practising case interviews. It is not unheard of for candidates to have done more than 100 practise cases before an interview. I would recommend a minimum of practising 20 case interviews before the real one.

One of my favourite resources for practising case interviews is PrepLounge.com. Here you can try solving cases of varying difficulties with classmates sitting next to you or other candidates from anywhere in the world via video call. They also have resources from practising your mathematics and brain teasers.

Scenarios to Watch Out For

Independence of Quantity Sold and Variable Cost

One situation to bear in mind that occasionally catches candidates out is when the variable cost does not necessarily correlate with the number of products sold.

One scenario where this phenomenon can occur is with a subscription-based business model. In this case, your variable cost structure should look like this, additionally considering customer utilisation:

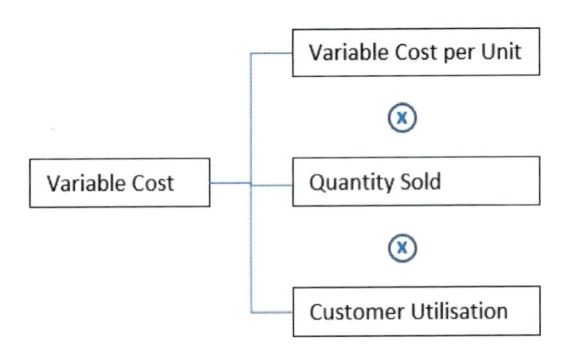

Figure 14: Variable Cost Segmentation for Subscription Business Model

Take, for instance, a yoga class subscription business that provides one class per week for a yearly price. The variable cost is dependent on how costly it is to run a session every week for each person, how many subscriptions are sold, and what percentage of weeks are used on average.

The Mix Effect

The mix effect commonly comes up in profitability cases when the client sees a reduction in their profit margin. The client at this stage may, in fact, also be experiencing declining revenues; however, they could also be flat or even increasing.

A common root cause of this issue is a proportional change in the mix of products sold by the client. If the client has started selling proportionally more of a lower-margin product, the firm's overall profit margin will decrease, no matter whether they are selling more or fewer products overall.

The product mix effect demonstrates why it is so important to drill down further into an area that may be causing an issue. In the case of product mix, you may observe an increasing quantity of sales. Do not stop there however, segment the sales and understand what specific products are doing well and which are doing less well. It may be the root cause of the issue.

3
ESTIMATION QUESTIONS

The additional part of the strategy consulting interview, either used as part of a case or separate, is estimation questions. These questions, composed of asking a candidate a seemingly impossible number to calculate, are designed to assess how well a candidate can structure their thinking and use logic and their own knowledge to come to a reasonable approximation.

The two types of questions asked can be categorised into either geometric estimation questions or market sizing. Each has a best-practice method in solving them which we shall discuss below.

The one thing to bear in mind when doing estimation questions is to make the mathematics easy for yourself. As long as you can justify them, pick numbers that are easy to work with and round alternatively after calculations. You don't need to put yourself in the position where you need to divide 379.3 by 17 without a calculator. (You won't have one).

Geometric Estimation Questions

The first type of estimation question asked by consulting interviewers are geometric estimation questions. These questions are designed to assess how comfortable you are with large numbers and how well you can break down a problem into its component parts.

Questions typically ask, "How many {small objects} can fit into a {big object}?". Favourites I have heard include; "How many ping-pong balls fit inside a Boeing 747 aeroplane?", "How many bananas fit inside a shipping crate?" and "How many stones makeup Brighton Beach?".

These may seem like impossible numbers to calculate; however, through applying a structured methodology, you will be able to come to a reasonable answer quite easily. The process I have found best is as follows:

1. Calculate Cross-Sectional Area of Large Object

A candidate should first calculate the cross-sectional area of the large object by taking an approximation of the width and multiplying it by an approximation of the height. Leverage your own experience and insight to explain why the numbers you give are a reasonable approximation. Use whatever unit is most appropriate here, but it is most often meters so the area would be meters squared.

Often candidates will also be dealing with large objects resembling cylinders, such as aeroplanes or tunnels. In this case, calculate the cylinder as if it had a square cross-section and then multiply that number by 0.8. (The area of a circle inside a square is 0.79 times the area of the square).

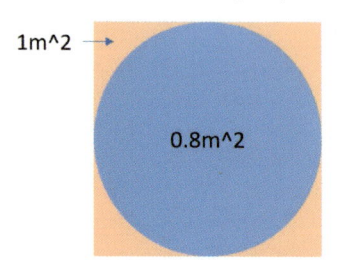

1m^2

0.8m^2

2. Estimate Length of Large Object to Calculate Volume

The next step is to take the cross-sectional area you have just calculated and multiply it by an estimated length of the large object. Again, use your own knowledge to bring context to why you believe it to be that length. Now you have the volume of the large object in, whichever unit you have chosen, cubed.

3. Calculate the Height and Width of the Small Object

At this stage, the candidate should now approximate the height and width of the small object.

These objects will typically be somewhere between 50cm and 1mm across their longest length so candidates should be comfortable with estimating those kinds of dimensions. A good starting point is to know that most adult's fingers are around 2cm wide. You can use this as a visual cue to guess that for example, a golf ball is 5cm high.

4. Calculate How Many Small Objects Fits Across the Y-Axis of the {Large Unit} Cube.

The candidate should now calculate the number of small objects that fit across one {unit} square vertically. First, convert the square height to the measurement unit of the small object, for example, 1 meter to 100 cm. Then divide the square height (100cm) by the height of the small object (5cm for a golf ball). The result (20) is the number of small objects that would fit along the vertical length of the meter cube.

5. Calculate How Many Small Objects Fits Across the X-Axis of the {Large Unit} Cube

This process is then repeated for the width of the small object to calculate how many would fit along the horizontal length of the cube (again 20 for the golf ball).

6. Calculate How Many Small Objects Fits Across the Z-Axis of the {Large Unit} Cube

The process is repeated for the last time for the length of the small object.

7. Calculate Number of Small Objects in a {Large Unit} Cube

The three numbers for how many small objects fit along one {large unit} along their Y, X and Z axis are multiplied to give the number of small objects fitting inside the volume unit used to calculate the size of the large object.

8. Final Calculation

The last step is to multiply the number of small objects fitting inside the {large unit} cube with the volume of the large object. This calculation will provide the answer to the number of small objects that fit inside the large object.

Example: "How many golf balls would fit inside a Boeing 747 passenger plane?"

1. I estimate that the height of a passenger plane is 4 meters as an adult is approximately 1.5 meters tall, and they have some space above their head to make 2 meters. The height is then doubled to account for the hold bellow where luggage is stored.

I estimate the width is also 4 meters as passenger planes generally resemble a cylindrical shape with a similar height and width.

The cross-sectional area as a square is therefore 4*4 = 16 meters squared. I multiply this by 0.8 as it is a circular cross-section to give 12.8 meters squared, which we round up to 13.

2. I then estimate the length of the passenger plane to be approximately 50 meters long given the

COMPONENTS & CONDITIONS

747 is one of the largest passenger planes, a seat most likely taking up about 1 meter from front to back, combined with the assumption of approximately 50 seats given that seat numbers usually go up to 35-40 on the smaller, more common passenger planes.

I then multiply our 13 meters squared cross-section by our 50-meter length to give 650 cubic meters as the passenger plane's volume.

3. I then estimate the height, or diameter in this case, of the golf ball to be approximately 5cm.

4. I convert the meter squared unit we used to measure the passenger plane to our golf ball unit of centimetres to give 100cm. I then divide this 100cm by our 5cm golf ball length to give 20, the number of golf balls that would fit along the y-axis of a meter cube.

As the small object is spherical, it will have the same height, width and length and will, therefore, fit the same number of times across the X, Y and Z axis of a meter cube.

5. I then multiple the answers to how many times the golf ball fits across the X, Y and Z axis. In this case, all three answers are 20.

20*20*20 = 8,000 golf balls in a meter square.

6. Finally, I can multiply the 8,000 by the volume of the passenger plane, 650, to give the answer of 5,200,000 golf balls fitting in a Boeing 747 passenger plane.

Market Sizing

The second type of estimation question you are likely to be given in a strategy consulting interview is market sizing. This type of question generally refers either, to the annual (occasionally weekly or daily) consumption or production of a particular product or, to the current number of a certain thing in existence.

Examples I have heard include; "How many cats are there in the UK?", "How many umbrellas are sold in the UK each year?" and "What length of spaghetti is eaten in Europe every year?".

For all market sizing estimation questions, there are two approaches you can adopt. These are referred to as a 'top-down' approach or 'bottom-up' approach. A top-down approach starts at the largest relevant number. For our "How many cats in the UK?" question, this would be the UK population. From there the candidate would gradually make the number smaller and smaller until they arrive at their answer.

The alternative 'bottom-up' approach moves in the opposite direction, starting at the smallest relevant number and builds up, growing the number until they arrive at the answer. For the same example, a candidate would start by guessing how many cats a cat owner typically owns.

I have two tips for market sizing estimation questions that are worth considering:

Always Consider Replacement Cycle when Estimating Consumption or Production.

For these types of questions, it is important to consider that if you work out how many products are owned, this may not be the annual consumption or production of the product.

Take laptop sales in China as an example; after ending up with the number of laptops owned in China, you must remember to divide this by how often laptops are replaced on average (maybe three years in this case). This would then provide your final answer.

Quarters Rule of Demographic Segmentation

When market sizing, you will often need to segment a population according to demographic groups. To achieve rough demographic segmentation quickly, I recommend assuming an 80-year life expectancy and even distribution, a reasonable approximation for developed countries and then segmenting this into the four age brackets of 0-20, 21-40, 41-60 and 61-80.

This method has the two benefits of being simple to compute the segment sizes on paper, simply halving the population twice, and being a good representation of various life stages: 0-20 = childhood and education, 21-40 = early career, 41-60 = late-career, 61-80 = retirement.

If the demographic segmentation is one of the pillar stones of the analysis, a candidate can accomplish a more detailed segmentation by halving the population a third time to analyse each age group by decade (0-10, 11-20, 21-30, 31-40, 41-50, 51-60, 61-70, 71-80).

Example: "How many iPads are sold in the UK every year?"

1. First, I take the UK population of approximately 60 million and segment it into eight this time as I imagine the demographic differences will be important. This gives 7.5 million people in each age group.

2. I then assign estimated percentages of iPad owner to each age group: 0-10 – 10%, 11-20 – 20%, 21-30 – 30%, 31-40 - 30%, 41-50 – 20%, 51-60 – 10%, 61-70 – 10%, 71-80 – 0%.

3. Multiplying each 7.5 million age group by their percentage ownership and summing the answers brings total UK iPad owners to an estimated 9.75 million people. Assuming that the vast majority of this use only one iPad, we can also assume that the number of iPads owned in the UK is 9.75 million. At this point, I would round up to 10 million, citing the minority of users owning multiple iPads to justify the increase.

4. The replacement cycle for an iPad can now be estimated. Either 2 or 3 years would be a reasonable number. Taking 2 years for this example, I would then divide 10 million by 2, giving 5 million iPads sold in the UK each year as the answer

5
GENERAL TIPS

Although there is plenty of advice out there, I thought it would be helpful to share what has worked well for me.

Case Competitions / Workshops to Differentiate and Network

Case competitions are essentially competitive case interview challenges solved as part of a team. They are usually held by a university and are a fantastic (and fun) way to practise business problem-solving technique in a slightly different environment. Furthermore, these competitions are a great way to differentiate yourself from other candidates, especially if you end up winning and can provide the opportunity to network with some of the largest consulting firms.

In addition, if you are studying at one of the target universities for these firms, case interview workshops will often be organised on campus which I highly recommend attending.

Become Comfortable with Your Story and Key Experiences

Outside of case interviews, either as part of initial screening or in the final partner interview, the consulting firm will want to ask you slightly more behavioural questions to gauge your qualities outside of core problem-solving. They will want to know things like your general background, why you're interested in consulting, what you enjoy doing, how you think you can develop, key examples of your various attributes and so on.

Being able to tell a clear and concise story helps enormously in persuading the interviewer that you are the right person for the job. To achieve this, I would advise taking some time to think about and structure a clear story for how you have come to apply to strategy consulting along with 4-5 key experiences that show your positive attributes. After practising these short explanations with friends and in mock interviews, your ability to draw on examples and describe them clearly will improve.

I recommend using the STAR model (situation-task-action-result) to help organise these examples.

6
EXAMPLE CASE

Southern Stationery

Interviewer: Your client is Southern Stationery, a large American stationary brand selling pens, pencils, erasers and rulers. Over the last year, they have seen a decline in their net profits. They want to understand why their profits are declining and what they can do to fix this problem.

Candidate: Thank you, that's an interesting problem. To check I've understood correctly; the client is Southern Stationery, an American company that sells stationery such as pencils and rulers and they want to know why their profits are declining and how they can improve this?

Interviewer: Correct

Candidate: Are there any other objectives other than improving profitability?

Interviewer: No

Candidate: I have one clarifying question if that's okay?

Interviewer: Sure

Candidate: What market does Southern Stationary sell to? For example, is it only US customers or do they sell internationally and I assume it's B-2-C primarily?

Interviewer: The client only sells their product within the US, and yes, they sell to individual consumers, through a variety of brick and mortar retail stores.

COMPONENTS & CONDITIONS

Information:
- Client = Southern Stationary (USA)
- Products = Pencils, rulers, erasers tec.
- Last year saw decline in net profits.

Objective: Find out why net profits have dropped / recommend solution.

Problem Solving Structure (Framework / Issue Tree):

Calculations:

Recommendation:

Candidate: Okay, great. Is it okay if I take a couple of minutes to structure my thoughts?

Interviewer: Of course, go ahead.

EDWARD VERNON

Objective: Find out why net profits have dropped / recommend solution.

Problem Solving Structure (Framework / Issue Tree):

Issue tree breaking down Profit into Revenue and Cost. Revenue splits into Average Price of Product and Quantity Sold. Cost splits into Variable Cost and Fixed Cost. Variable Cost branches into Materials and Labour. Labour branches into Hourly Rate (circled) and Number of Employees, highlighting P-HI. A callout box reads: "Increase in Average Hourly Rate During F/Y 2018".

Information:
- Client = Southern Stationary (USA)
- Products = Pencils, rulers, erasers tec.
- Last year saw decline in net profits.

Calculations: ↶

Recommendation:

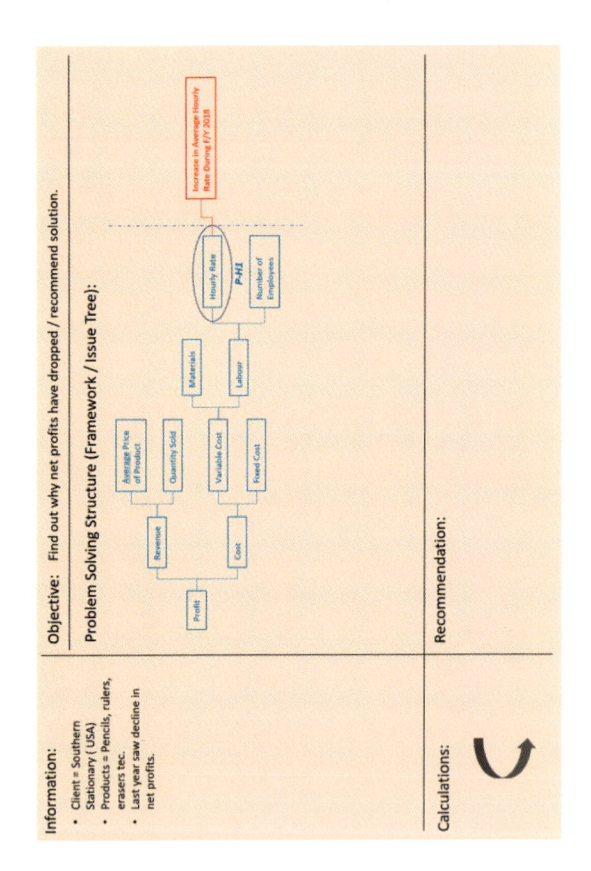

Candidate: Just to walk you through my thinking; I've split the client's profitability issue into its component parts of revenue and cost and again into price, quantity, variable cost and fixed cost. Going off my own knowledge of stationary being fairly commodity-like with a fairly stable price and demand, my initial hypothesis is that the reduced net profits are caused by a cost issue. Specifically, I'd like to look at variable labour costs first as I understand trade unions are fairly strong in the US so this may be causing the issue.

Firstly, is this stationary manufactured in the US?

Interviewer: The raw materials are sourced from overseas, but yes, all manufacturing is done in the US.

Candidate: Why is all manufacturing done in the US?

Interviewer: The Southern Stationary brand is built on the 'American-Made' slogan.

Candidate: I'd therefore like to ask if you have the average information on the hourly rate of the American manufacturing workers over the last three years.

Interviewer: Of course. The hourly rate has stayed at $9 per hour over this period.

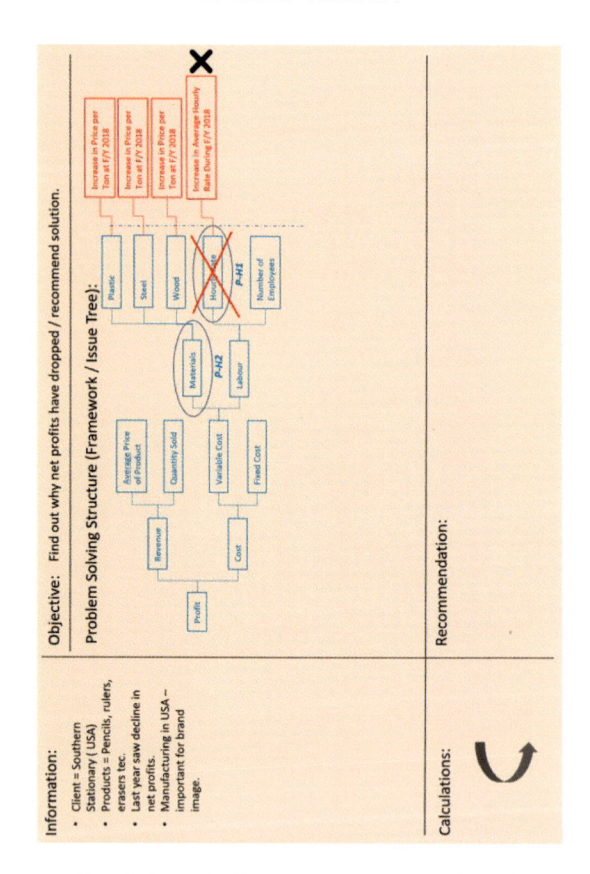

Objective: Find out why net profits have dropped / recommend solution.

Problem Solving Structure (Framework / Issue Tree):

[Issue tree diagram with branches: Profit → Revenue (Average Price of Product, Quantity Sold) and Cost (Variable Cost → Materials [Plastic, Steel, Wood] and Labour [Hourly Rate (P-H1, crossed out), Number of Employees]; Fixed Cost). P-H2 circles Materials. Red annotations: Increase in Price per Ton at F/Y 2018 (×3), Increase in Average Hourly Rate During F/Y 2018 (marked with X).]

Information:
- Client = Southern Stationary (USA)
- Products = Pencils, rulers, erasers tec.
- Last year saw decline in net profits.
- Manufacturing in USA – important for brand image.

Calculations:

↶

Recommendation:

Candidate: In that case, I revise my hypothesis that it is actually a material cost problem, causing the low profitability. Do you have any information on the cost per ton of for the raw plastic, metal and wood, you use in the stationary products over the last three years?

COMPONENTS & CONDITIONS

Interviewer: Yes, I do. Here is a table:

	2016	2017	2018
Wood ($ per ton)	2,423	2,411	2,432
Plastic ($ per ton)	5,875	5,872	7,320
Steel ($ per ton)	12,321	12,259	12,304

Candidate: Thank you. So immediately, I can see that the price of your plastic raw material has increased. Is this a significant material for the products you manufacture?

Interviewer: Yes, plastics account for approximately 70% of material usage.

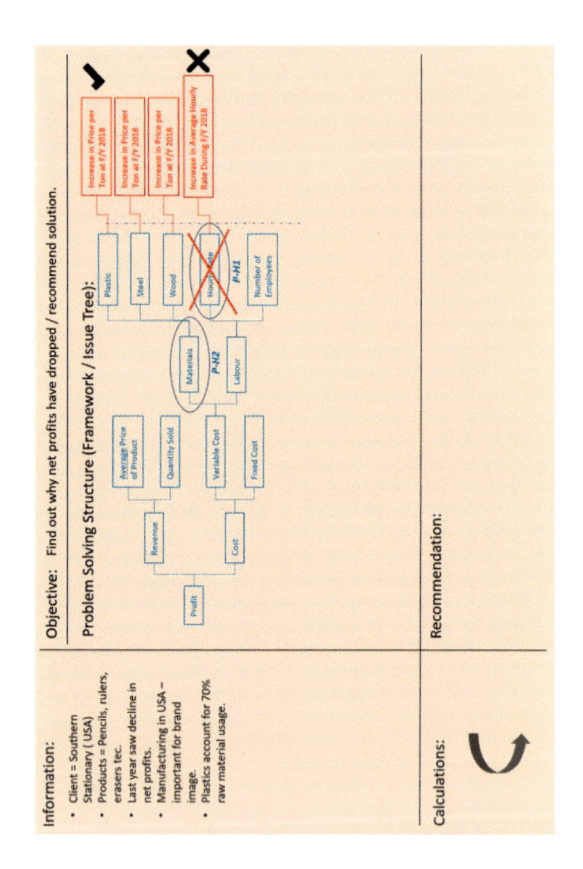

Objective: Find out why net profits have dropped / recommend solution.

Problem Solving Structure (Framework / Issue Tree):

[Diagram: Issue tree with Profit branching into Revenue (Average Price of Product, Quantity Sold) and Cost (Variable Cost, Fixed Cost). Variable Cost branches into Materials (P-N2, circled) and Labour. Materials branches into Plastic, Steel, Wood, House Rate (P-H1, crossed out), Number of Employees. Linked to orange boxes: Increase in Price per Ton at F/Y 2018, Increase in Price per Ton at F/Y 2018, Increase in Price per Ton at F/Y 2018, Increase in Average Hourly Rate During F/Y 2018.]

Information:
- Client = Southern Stationary (USA)
- Products = Pencils, rulers, erasers tec.
- Last year saw decline in net profits.
- Manufacturing in USA – important for brand image.
- Plastics account for 70% raw material usage.

Calculations:

Recommendation:

Candidate: In that case, I believe I have found your root cause of the decrease in profits. The increased cost of the primary manufacturing material, plastic, in 2018 has cut into the variable costs for that year.

Now I'd like to understand how this problem can

COMPONENTS & CONDITIONS

be resolved. Firstly, has there been a change in the specifications of this plastic or a change in supplier?

Interviewer: The specifications for the plastic are the same; however, at the end of 2017, the client's supplier, Texas Plastics merged with Salt Lake Chemicals to become Texalt Co.

Candidate: Okay, that makes sense. It seems as if the new merger has increased the supplier power of the plastics, allowing them to charge higher prices. Are there any alternative plastics suppliers the client can switch to?

Interviewer: Unfortunately not, Texalt Co. is the only company able to provide the required plastic at the quantity we require.

EDWARD VERNON

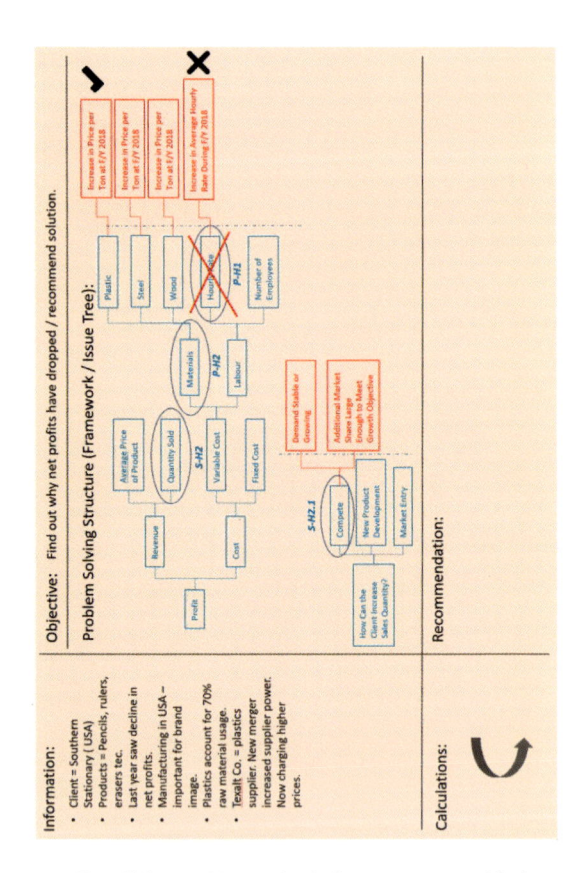

Information:
- Client = Southern Stationary (USA)
- Products = Pencils, rulers, erasers tec.
- Last year saw decline in net profits.
- Manufacturing in USA – important for brand image.
- Plastics account for 70% raw material usage.
- Texalt Co. = plastics supplier. New merger increased supplier power. Now charging higher prices.

Objective: Find out why net profits have dropped / recommend solution.

Problem Solving Structure (Framework / Issue Tree):

Profit
├── Revenue
│   ├── Average Price of Product
│   └── Quantity Sold *(S-H2)*
└── Cost
    ├── Variable Cost
    │   ├── Materials *(P-H2)*
    │   │   ├── Plastic — Increase in Price per Ton at F/Y 2018 ✓
    │   │   ├── Steel — Increase in Price per Ton at F/Y 2018 ✗
    │   │   ├── Wood — Increase in Price per Ton at F/Y 2018
    │   │   └── Hourly Rate *(P-H1)* ✗ — Increase in Average Hourly Rate During F/Y 2018
    │   └── Labour
    │   └── Number of Employees
    └── Fixed Cost

How Can the Client Increase Sales Quantity? *(S-H2.1)*
- Compete — Demand Stable or Growing; Additional Market Share Large Enough to Meet Growth Objective
- New Product Development
- Market Entry

Calculations:

Recommendation:

Candidate: Given the information provided so far, regarding the merger and the 'American-made' branding, I believe that the best way to improve our client's net profits would be to increase the revenue profit component to account for the additional costs rather than cut costs elsewhere.

COMPONENTS & CONDITIONS

Firstly, I'd like to understand whether it would be most effective for the client to grow their market share with their current product and market or grow into different areas. I'd first like to look at the less extreme option of competing in the current product and market. Do you have any information on US market size for stationary over the last 3 years?

Interviewer: Yes, it is approximately $750 million per year every year since 2016.

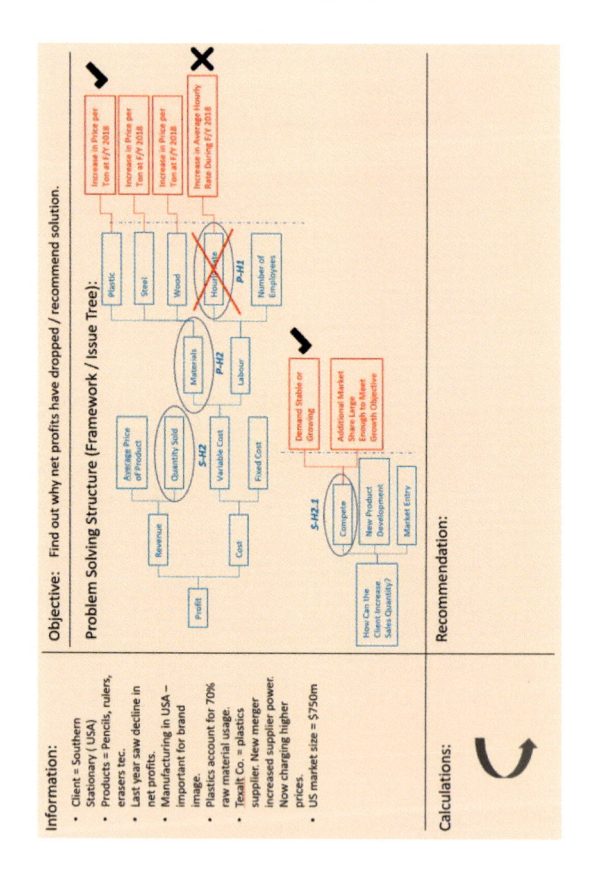

Objective: Find out why net profits have dropped / recommend solution.

Problem Solving Structure (Framework / Issue Tree):

- Profit
  - Revenue
    - Average Price of Product
    - Quantity Sold — *S-H2*
  - Cost
    - Variable Cost
      - Materials — *P-H2*
        - Plastic ✓ (Increase in Price per Ton at F/Y 2018)
        - Steel (Increase in Price per Ton at F/Y 2018)
        - Wood (Increase in Price per Ton at F/Y 2018)
        - ~~House Hold~~ ✗ (Increase in Average Hourly Rate During F/Y 2018) — *P-H1*
      - Labour
        - Number of Employees
    - Fixed Cost
  - How Can the Client Increase Sales Quantity?
    - Compete — *S-H2.1* ✓
      - Demand Stable or Growing
      - Additional Market Share Large Enough to Meet Growth Objective
    - New Product Development
    - Market Entry

Information:
- Client = Southern Stationary (USA)
- Products = Pencils, rulers, erasers tec.
- Last year saw decline in net profits.
- Manufacturing in USA – important for brand image.
- Plastics account for 70% raw material usage.
- Texalt Co. = plastics supplier. New merger increased supplier power. Now charging higher prices.
- US market size = $750m

Calculations:

↻

Recommendation:

Candidate: Thank you. And what have the client's revenues been over the last 3 years?

Interviewer: $340 million in 2016, $345 million in 2017 and $342million in 2018.

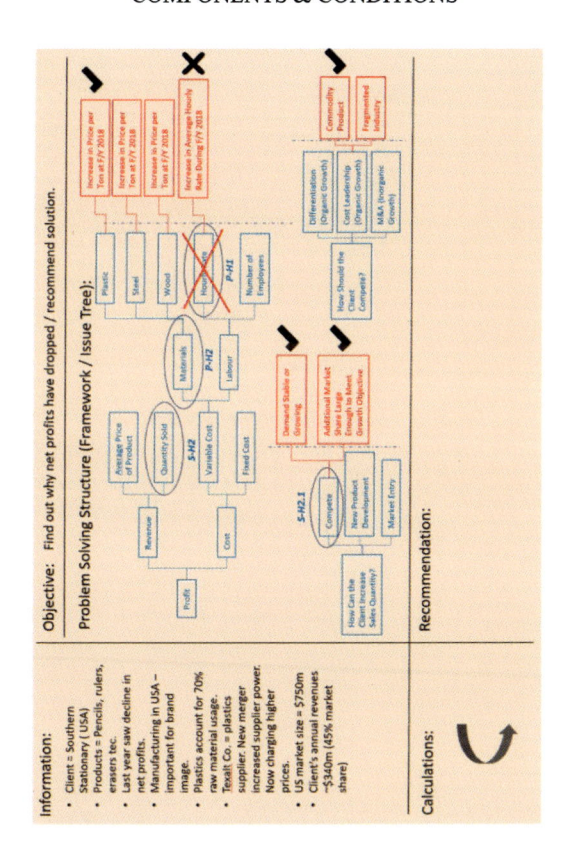

COMPONENTS & CONDITIONS

Objective: Find out why net profits have dropped / recommend solution.

Problem Solving Structure (Framework / Issue Tree):

[Issue tree diagram with the following elements:]

- Profit branches into Revenue and Cost
- Revenue → Average Price of Product, Quantity Sold (S-H2)
  - Average Price of Product → Plastic, Steel, Wood, Rubber (crossed out), Number of Employees (P-H1) [crossed out]
    - Increase in Price per Ton at F/Y 2018
    - Increase in Price per Ton at F/Y 2018
    - Increase in Price per Ton at F/Y 2018
    - Increase in Average Hourly Rate During F/Y 2018
- Cost → Variable Cost (P-H2), Fixed Cost
  - Variable Cost → Materials, Labour
- Quantity Sold (S-H2) → How Can the Client Increase Sales Quantity?
  - Compete (S-H2.1), New Product Development, Market Entry
    - Compete → Demand Stable or Growing, Addressable Market Share Large Enough to Meet Growth Objective
- How Should the Client Compete? → Differentiation (Organic Growth), Cost Leadership (Organic Growth), M&A (Inorganic Growth)
  - Commodity Product, Fragmented Industry

Information:
- Client = Southern Stationary (USA)
- Products = Pencils, rulers, erasers tec.
- Last year saw decline in net profits.
- Manufacturing in USA – important for brand image.
- Plastics account for 70% raw material usage.
- Texalt Co. = plastics supplier. New merger increased supplier power. Now charging higher prices.
- US market size = $750m
- Client's annual revenues ~$340m (45% market share)

Calculations:

↩

Recommendation:

Candidate: Okay, so the client has a significant market share. Who are their major competitors and what are their market shares?

Interviewer: All other competitors are fairly small, with annual revenues at no more than $5 million.

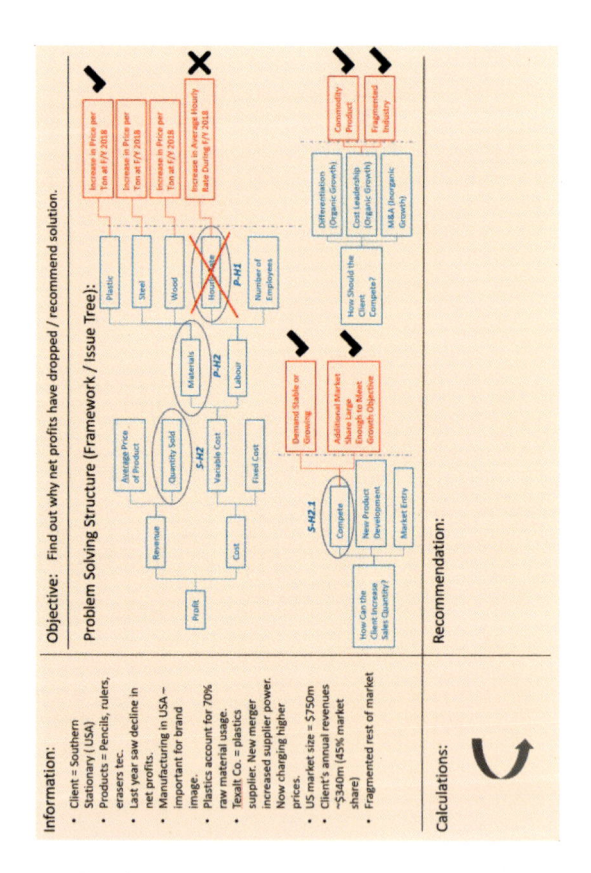

Candidate: Okay, brilliant so I think I have a recommendation for the client. Can I take a minute to bring together and synthesise my thoughts?

Interviewer: Of course, take your time.

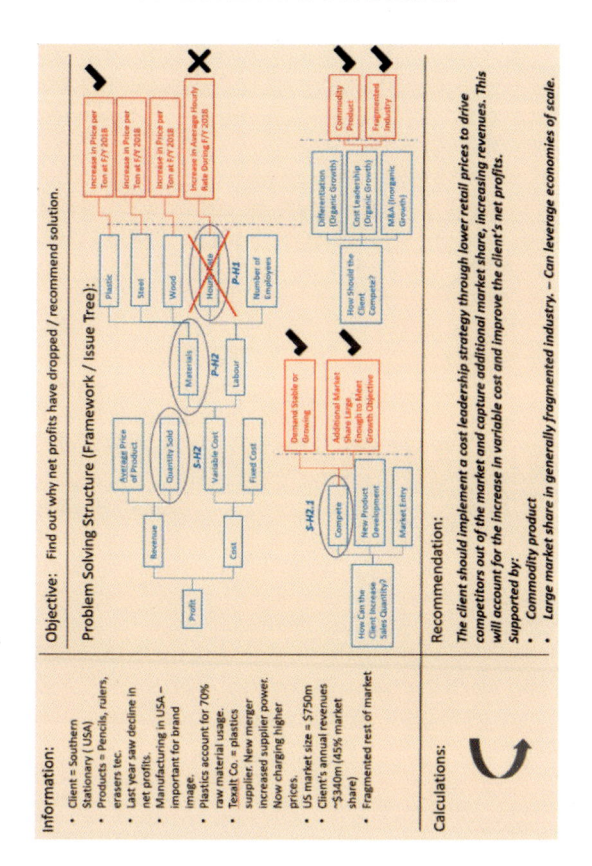

COMPONENTS & CONDITIONS

Objective: Find out why net profits have dropped / recommend solution.

Problem Solving Structure (Framework / Issue Tree):

[Issue tree diagram with the following elements:]

- Profit
  - Revenue
    - Average Price of Product
      - Increase in Price per Ton e/Y 2016
      - Increase in Price per Ton e/Y 2018
      - Increase in Price per Ton at f/Y 2018
      - Increase in Average Hourly Rate During F/Y 2018 ✗
    - Quantity Sold — **S-H2**
      - Materials — **P-H2**
        - Plastic
        - Steel
        - Wood
        - Household ✗ — **P-H1**
      - Labour
        - Number of Employees
  - Cost
    - Variable Cost
    - Fixed Cost
- Compete — **S-H2.1**
  - New Product Development
  - Market Entry
  - Demand Stable or Growing
  - Additional Market Share Large Enough to Meet Growth Objective
- How Can the Client Increase Sales Quantity?
- How should the Client Compete?
  - Differentiation (Organic Growth)
  - Cost Leadership (Organic Growth)
  - M&A (Inorganic Growth)
  - Commodity Product
  - Fragmented Industry

Information:
- Client = Southern Stationary (USA)
- Products = Pencils, rulers, erasers tec.
- Last year saw decline in net profits.
- Manufacturing in USA – important for brand image.
- Plastics account for 70% raw material usage.
- Texalt Co. = plastics supplier. New merger increased supplier power. Now charging higher prices.
- US market size = $750m
- Client's annual revenues ~$340m (45% market share)
- Fragmented rest of market

Calculations:

Recommendation:

The client should implement a cost leadership strategy through lower retail prices to drive competitors out of the market and capture additional market share, increasing revenues. This will account for the increase in variable cost and improve the client's net profits.

Supported by:
- Commodity product
- Large market share in generally fragmented industry. – Can leverage economies of scale.

Candidate: As we've discussed, the client is experiencing decreased net profits due to a recent merger in their primary materials supplier who are now charging their customers more. Unfortunately, this supplier cannot be changed due to the client's quantity requirements.

In order to keep manufacturing in the US, my recommendation would be to account for the increasing costs through capturing additional sales from the market through a cost leadership strategy. As the product is fairly commodity-like and the rest of the market is fragmented, the client could leverage their economies of scale to bring their retail price below the break-even point of their competitors, capturing additional customers.

This is why I would advise the client to lower their prices gradually until smaller competitors start to close down, and their customers become the client's customers. Net profits may decrease further initially; however, they should rebound beyond initial levels following the competitor closures.

If I were to have more time, I would look at what additional market share the client would need to capture to regain the original level of profitability. I would then form a group of the companies with the weakest profit margins the client would be able to target with a cost leadership strategy and understand how much they would have to reduce their retail prices by to drop below the break-even point of this group.

REFERENCES:

Nogueira, B. (2017). The 5 Ways to be MECE in Case Interviews – Crafting Cases. [online] Crafting Cases. Available at: https://www.craftingcases.com/the-5-ways-to-be-mece/ [Accessed 2 Oct. 2019].

ABOUT THE AUTHOR

Edward Vernon is a practising strategy consultant based in London. He advises the executive teams of international corporations and governments on their long-term strategic challenges along with their innovation and transformation strategy. He holds a Master of Science degree from Imperial College London in Innovation, Entrepreneurship & Management and has prior experience spanning venture capital and mechanical engineering.

Notes:

Notes:

Notes:

Notes: